Eyes on Jesus

Psalm 23—A Guide to Overcoming the
Worry and Stress in Our Lives and Culture

Jeff Simmons

Sermon To Book
www.sermontobook.com

Eyes on Jesus / Jeff Simmons
ISBN-13: 978-1-952602-46-7

Eyes on Jesus is a must-read for everyone searching for how to deal with worry and stress in this life. Often, our anxiety is rooted in "not enough" fears. Fears that say: "I am not enough." "I have not done enough." "There will not be enough (safety, time, money, love, etc.)." Our culture has been struggling with pervasive, chronic anxiety for many years, and then in 2020–2021, we saw unprecedented levels of suffering, loss, and isolation. Everyone across the globe experienced pain and loss at some level.

We have been resilient and strong and brave, beyond measure. And yet, this does not come without a cost. We must not be naïve. The body truly does keep the score. Some may have had moments of denial or shock, and they may have moments where adrenaline and anxiety were high, or even a sense of dread. Some had moments of feeling helpless, fatigued, or depressed. Something of this magnitude has the ability to shake our foundations and disrupt many of the things we have built our lives on.

Or, with the right resources, support, and trust in the Lord, it can create tremendous growth in our lives and anchor us deeper in our faith. Stress and trauma can shrink our window of tolerance. We need permission to be honest when we are struggling. We need to know we can get support from our partners, church, and friends. We all need strategies to recalibrate, and we need to look for meaning in our loss and trials. It will give us comfort to know that "this matters," and "I can use this experience to grow and to help others." We can trust that God truly has a purpose in the pain. This book is about you being the healthiest, emotionally and spiritually, that you can be, so that you can live a life of freedom and peace, knowing in and through Christ, there is always "enough."

Amy Alexander, LMFT
Executive Director, The Refuge Center for Counseling

As an anxious person by nature, I have read many articles and books on the subject of anxiety. Jeff Simmons gets right to the root cause by opening our hearts to Psalm 23. This book will not put you to sleep but will certainly help you sleep better.

Mike Minter
Pastor Emeritus, Reston Bible Church in Sterling, VA

Jeff Simmons is a trusted voice in our community, across the globe, and as a friend to me. He has a unique way of illuminating truth and offering it with profound honesty, grace, and kindness, all at the same time. I'm grateful for his work, his heart, and his words in this book, *Eyes on Jesus*. I believe we'll all know Jesus better, and know more of what it means to fix our eyes on the source of grace, hope, and contentment, as a result of reading this book.

Sissy Goff, M.Ed, LPC-MHSP, CCATP
Director of Child & Adolescent Counseling, Daystar Counseling Ministries, Inc.

Eyes on Jesus is a personal invitation to walk through one of the best-known and most-loved passages in Holy Scripture. Pastor Jeff Simmons shepherds the reader through the hills and valleys of the Shepherd's psalm with his unwavering faith and confidence in a loving Heavenly Father who never leaves us, never forsakes us, and always finds a way. All who take this walk with Jeff will find themselves challenged, strengthened, and growing in their personal conviction of the goodness of God!

Wayne Williams
Senior Pastor, Renew Church in Waco, Texas

Eyes on Jesus is a must-read for everyone searching for how to deal with worry and stress in this life. This book will open your eyes to see what Jesus wants to do in your heart and life. Get ready to be challenged and inspired.

Kathy Koon
Counseling Director, Rolling Hills Community Church

In our work with pastors and pastoral couples, we rarely find anyone with stronger shepherding gifts than Jeff Simmons. So, it makes all the sense that Jeff would write a book based on the Good Shepherd and use David's words to encourage and shepherd every reader to focus their eyes on Jesus. Whatever season you find yourself in, this book will provide encouragement and hope, as well as the space for personal and written reflection. In the words of Richard of Chichester, as you read this book, allow Jeff to shepherd you "to see Jesus more clearly, love Him more dearly, and follow Him more nearly."

Jeff and Lora Helton
Life & Executive Coaches, WellSpring Coaching & Training

Life is filled with hills and valleys where stress and worry often creep into your everyday routine without notice. *Eyes on Jesus* encourages you to boldly walk in peace with the assurance that the Lord is always there to calm your spirit and refresh your soul.

Connia Nelson
Senior Vice President and Chief Human Resources Officer, Lifeway Christian Resources

Jeff's personal relationship with the Lord Jesus is evident in his life and in this wonderfully practical explanation of this reassuring psalm, which comes at a time that we desperately need it. Insightful, with wisdom that can be easily applied in our daily lives, *Eyes on Jesus* includes challenging questions and action steps which are perfect for individual reflection, couples interaction, or small group discussion and application.

Pike Williams, LMFT
The Refuge Center for Counseling

Special Thanks

This book is dedicated to Jesus Christ, the Good Shepherd. My prayer is that we can all learn to keep our eyes on Him. He is the One who will provide for and protect us all. Our worth and value come in Christ Jesus alone. May God grow us deeply in Christ and use each of us in a mighty way for His glory. We are the sheep of His pasture. We can take great delight in knowing that the Lord is our shepherd and we lack nothing.

After the Lord, I would like to dedicate this book to the incredible people of God's flock at Rolling Hills Community Church. We are truly a part of something bigger than ourselves at Rolling Hills, something only our God can do. Our God is writing an incredible story in His Church, and I love being on this journey with every person who calls Rolling Hills home. I also love serving our God with our amazing staff team! We have seen our God do miracles, and I truly believe that our best days are still ahead as we keep our eyes on Jesus. I love all my brothers and sisters in Christ at Rolling Hills.

I also want to thank Jennifer Milligan, Rebecca Ahlstrom, and everyone else who helped to bring this book to life. Thank you! May our God use this book to draw each of us close to His heart as we follow the Good Shepherd.

Additionally, I want to thank my amazing wife, Lisa. We have been married for twenty years, and each day, I love

her more. We are so blessed, and I love following Jesus together.

Finally, to our three beautiful girls, Grace, Mabry, and Kate— I pray that each of you keeps your eyes on Jesus all the days of your life. God has incredible plans for each of you, and I am so proud to be your dad.

—Jeff Simmons

CONTENTS

A Pandemic of the Heart

The LORD is my shepherd, I lack nothing. He makes me lie down in green pastures, he leads me beside quiet waters, he refreshes my soul. He guides me along the right paths for his name's sake. Even though I walk through the darkest valley, I will fear no evil, for you are with me; your rod and your staff, they comfort me.

You prepare a table before me in the presence of my enemies. You anoint my head with oil; my cup overflows. Surely your goodness and love will follow me all the days of my life, and I will dwell in the house of the LORD forever.
—Psalm 23

Do you ever have one of those nights when your mind is racing because there's so much going on in your life, and you're trying so hard to figure everything out that you can't seem to shut your mind down? We have all been there. There are times when we can't sleep because of worry, or because we are trying to figure out how we can possibly get everything done. One hiccup in our plans, and our stress levels go up. We run all sorts of scenarios in our minds trying to figure out the best way forward or account for all the ways things might go wrong.

Meanwhile, the minutes and hours continue to pass by as we lie there in bed, not sleeping. Then 4 a.m. comes around, and we think, "I'm not getting any sleep anyway, so I may as well be answering emails or doing something else productive."

But come 10 a.m., we receive an email or text saying something like, "Hey, everything's fine! We're on track. Everyone is all good."

We are relieved, of course, but we also think, "Why didn't I sleep? What was the point of all that worrying, stress, and anxiety?"

This isn't a new experience for human beings. A quote—popularly attributed to French essayist Michel de Montaigne, who lived over four hundred years ago—says, "My life has been filled with terrible misfortunes, most of which never happened."[1] Our minds like to play out the worst-case scenarios, but the overwhelming majority of the things we worry about never come to fruition.

Yet we continue to worry. We're anxious, stressed, and afraid in a way that permeates our minds and hearts. Stress and worry can be detrimental to our physical health. Anxiety can produce symptoms like shortness of breath, sleeplessness, and panic attacks. For some people, anxiety and depression reach the level of serious clinical disorders. There is a pandemic of anxiety in our lives and our culture.

Beyond its impact on us as individuals, anxiety shapes the world in which our children are growing up. Amid our adult worries, we can easily forget how heavy the expectation to perform in school, on the ballfield, and in life in general is for children in our world today. The resulting anxiety about the consequences of falling short weighs on young people as well as adults.

Note that there is a difference between grounded fear, on the one hand, and anxiety, on the other. Healthy, well-founded fear occurs in response to an immediate situation, a moment for "fight or flight." Worry and anxiety, by contrast, are preemptive fear—that is, fear of hypothetical situations, of what could happen or might be.

We may think, "If I just had more money, it would solve all of my problems." We're tempted to think that we're just one raise, bonus, new job, or lottery win away from being worry-free. Sometimes we think that technology is the answer. In the United States, however, we already live in the wealthiest nation that's ever existed. In addition, in the United States, we're part of the most technologically advanced civilization the earth has ever seen. This raises the question, "Why are our stress and anxiety off the charts today?" The answer is: because wealth and technology will never solve all our problems.

It ultimately comes back to our hearts. God created us, and He wants us to have an ongoing, growing relationship with Him. God desires for us to develop a deep walk with Him and to become more passionate about what is dear to His heart. God wants the best life for us.

With this in mind, we're about to explore one of the most beautiful portions of Scripture in all of the Bible: Psalm 23. This is such a popular Bible chapter that you have probably heard it read at a church service, at a funeral, or in a hospital room. It offers deep reassurance and hope, even in the most difficult circumstances. In the words of the nineteenth-century preacher Charles Spurgeon, this brief chapter "has charmed more griefs to rest than all the philosophy of the world."[2] At the end of each chapter of this book, a workbook section will help you to turn your eyes on Jesus to receive His peace.

This beautiful scriptural passage was meant not only for those big moments in life, but also for our everyday journey. Psalm 23 speaks to our hearts and brings God's peace amid the worries and storms of life. This psalm points us to a deeper understanding of how we can experience the calm and peace our God so desires for each of us.

CHAPTER ONE

My Shepherd

The LORD is my shepherd, I lack nothing.
—Psalm 23:1

Imagine you're in your happy place, wherever that is for you—maybe the beach. It's a beautiful day, and you're lying on a hammock set up between two palm trees. Relaxing music is playing as gentle waves roll in. Your blood pressure is nice and settled.

But what if you change the music to the *Jaws* theme? Suddenly you're on alert, and your blood pressure goes through the roof as you scan the water for menacing fins. That's how quickly and dramatically anxiety can throw our hearts, minds, and lives into turmoil.

The Bible identifies Psalm 23 as a psalm of King David, the king who was known to be a man after God's own heart (Acts 13:22) because of the way he pursued the Lord. Though he was far from perfect, David loved God. After decades as king of Israel, David had accumulated wisdom through many victories, as well as through sorrows, many battles, failures, and other difficult experiences. David won many battles, but he also suffered major failures. In Psalm 23, David is pouring out his heart to God and passing along the lessons he learned to future generations, including us.

David sets the tone with his opening line, pouring out his heart in a powerful, passionate way: "The LORD is my shepherd, I lack nothing" (Psalm 23:1). Let's break this down.

"LORD" here, in caps, is the personal name for God, Yahweh (YHWH).[3] It's a name that speaks to God's sovereignty and power as the Creator,[4] yet it's also what God invites His people to call Him.

The verb "is" indicates the present tense of God in David's life and ours. He is not just a God who has been there in the past or will be there in the future. He *is* the God of the present, the God of our here and now.

God is present in a personal sense, as the personal pronoun "my" reflects. In this line, David wasn't describing God as the shepherd of Israel or of all humankind, but as *his* shepherd. And God longs to be our personal shepherd, too.

As for the word "shepherd," remember that long before David was a warrior and a king, he was a shepherd. He knew what it meant to herd sheep—to lead them and to care for them in a personal way that's far removed from modern scenes of men and dogs driving masses of sheep for shearing or slaughter. In fact, when young David made his case to King Saul that he could fight the enemy champion Goliath, he pointed out, "Your servant has been keeping his father's sheep" (1 Samuel 17:34–37). David was emphasizing his fearless commitment, putting his life on the line to protect the flock from lions and bears.

So, when David said, "The LORD is my shepherd" (Psalm 23:1), he was acknowledging God's lovingkindness and tenacity in caring for him as a shepherd takes care of his sheep, by being personally involved. That's what God does for us.

I Lack Nothing

Many of us sometimes wish for things we don't have, and we think that our lives would be better, our problems solved, if we had those things. But can you say right now that you lack anything truly necessary in your life? Do you lack basic food, clothing, or shelter?

You probably don't miss many meals for lack of food. When you go into your closet, it's likely that you're deciding *which* shirt you're going to wear, not looking to see *whether* you have a shirt to wear. There's a difference between needs and wants, as we all like to tell our kids when they say that they "need" the latest, trending gadget. As adults, we have to remember it, too.

David understood this. When he said, "I lack nothing," he meant that God met all of his needs. If the Lord is our shepherd and meets all of our needs, then why do we have so much stress and worry? Why does it permeate our lives?

His Still, Small Voice

You're far from alone if you struggle with anxiety. Throughout the Bible, we see real people who didn't have it all together any more than you or I do today.

Take the prophet Elijah, for instance. He was a man's man who seemed to embody everything a great prophet ought to be. One of his defining moments came when King Ahab and Queen Jezebel were leading Israel astray in worshiping the false god Baal (1 Kings 16:29–33).

Elijah was so bold that he challenged the four hundred and fifty prophets of Baal to a showdown on Mount Carmel (1 Kings 18:18–40). Amid some trash talk from Elijah—"Shout louder! ... Perhaps he [Baal] is deep in thought, or busy, or traveling" (1 Kings 18:27)—the prophets of Baal failed multiple times to coax their god to light the sacrificial altar they had built. Then, after a single prayer from Elijah, God consumed by fire the water-drenched altar and the bull sacrifices he had set up. Elijah won an incredible victory for God. He then killed the four hundred and fifty prophets of this false god and set Israel back on track to worship the one true God.

Seems like a terrific spiritual victory, right? But sometimes the enemy finds a foothold in our hearts right in the midst of our spiritual highs.

Elijah got word that Queen Jezebel was angry. You'd think that after defeating four hundred and fifty prophets, Elijah's response to her would have been along the lines of, "Bring it!" You might assume that he would have been even more emboldened after such a great victory. But instead, Elijah got scared and worried—so scared, in fact, that he ran for forty days and forty nights, then hid in a cave (1 Kings 19:1–9).

At this point, Elijah heard from God, who asked him, "What are you doing here, Elijah?" (1 Kings 19:9). At this, the prophet took the opportunity to unload his anxieties on God. He was worried that out of all Israel, he was alone in rejecting Baal and would be hunted and killed for his faithfulness to God (1 Kings 19:10). In response, God told Elijah to get ready because He was about to pass by the mountain (1 Kings 19:11).

God did come to Elijah on the mountain, but not in the way Elijah thought He would come. God was not in a powerful gust of wind or in an earthquake, but He appeared to Elijah in "a gentle whisper" (1 Kings 19:11–12). Some versions say "a still small voice" (NKJV). In this gentle voice, God told Elijah that his anxieties were misguided because, in fact, the prophet wasn't alone: seven thousand other Israelites had also refused to bow to Baal (1 Kings 19:18).

In this significant moment, why did God speak to Elijah in a whisper? If you're a parent, a grandparent, or an aunt or uncle, you may appreciate that when a child is anxious or scared, the best remedy is to draw the child close, offering words of comfort in a soothing voice. When Elijah heard that still, small voice, he remembered that God was there for him. And He is here for you, too.

From there, Elijah went back to serving God faithfully. It seems that he needed some time in the Lord's presence, mainly to quiet his anxieties. There's a great lesson here: God ministers to us His way. We also need time in His presence for Him to calm our fears and quiet our souls.

Learning to Trust Our Shepherd

So, how do we fight against the pandemic of anxiety in our lives and culture today? Let's begin by identifying some key, practical truths about dealing with unhealthy anxiety, worry, stress, and fear.

First, remember that He is God and you're not. David starts out Psalm 23 by declaring Him "the LORD." Anxiety and worry stem from us trying to be in control, but it is only God who is ultimately sovereign over all. Only He has that kind of power over circumstances. God created the world, and He created you, so He knows how you work. His plans for you are far bigger and better than anything you could imagine or make happen on your own! No matter what's going on in your life, God's not surprised. He has got it all handled. Trust Him!

God can bring healing to the anxiety, worry, and fear in your life. God *is*, and He is at work in your life, drawing you to Himself. Anxiety is physical, mental, and emotional, yes, and it must be addressed in a holistic way, but at its root, much of anxiety and worry is spiritual.

Don't try to face your struggle alone, as Elijah did, running off to hide in a cave. God often uses other people, such as friends, family members, pastors, and Christ-centered counselors, in our lives. Everybody's facing a battle in life, and though we may think that we've got it all figured out, it's important to open up and be honest with each other.

Yes, there's a time to seek the wisdom and input of a counselor. To some of us, it makes perfect sense to have coaches for baseball, basketball, or soccer when we're kids, but when it comes to life as adults, we think, "I'll figure it out on my own." A pastor or other counselor is a "coach" for marriage, parenting, or whatever other aspects of life are proving difficult—someone to share with and from whom we can receive a knowledgeable outside perspective.

In some cases, God can work through doctors and medicine in order to bring healing to anxiety and stress. Maybe your life feels like it's spiraling out of control in a way that goes beyond a difficult season, or maybe you have a family history of anxiety disorders. If necessary, by God's grace, you can find the right doctors, be prescribed the right medicines, and go through a treatment program to help you live a healthy, peaceful life. In the midst of medical remedies, God can achieve significant spiritual work in our hearts as He brings healing to our minds and bodies.

God meets us where we are. When you find yourself in dark places, remember that you are not alone. I don't know what exactly you, your children, or other people in your life are facing right now. However, I know beyond a doubt that with God, there's always hope. Hold on tightly to Him—because He *is*, and He is your shepherd. He is not just your family's shepherd or your country's shepherd, but *your* shepherd.

God longs to have a personal relationship with you through Jesus. That's why Jesus died on the cross! When you recognize your need for Him, you place your hope in

Him, giving Him your sins, your worries, your stress, and all the rest. When He becomes your personal Lord and Savior, He makes you new from the inside out. Then, having been saved, you follow Christ with your whole heart, seeking to become more like Jesus and less like the world every day.

Think about this: Jesus wasn't ever stressed out. Jesus wasn't ever in a hurry, and He was never afraid. Instead, Jesus taught us to put our trust in God and to focus on His presence in our minds and hearts.

Excessive worry is, essentially, practical atheism. Sure, God gave us the capacity for fear and anxiety, and in small doses, they can be healthy and helpful. Healthy fear is why we don't make a habit of strolling into bear dens or petting rattlesnakes. Healthy anxiety is sometimes what gets us off the couch so we can prepare for an important meeting or presentation. But excessive anxiety pushes God away so that as far as impacting our daily lives is concerned, He may as well not exist.

When we worry excessively, we are choosing not to trust God, in any kind of practical way, to take care of us. In John 10:11, Jesus declared, "I am the good shepherd." As our shepherd, He can be trusted with our very lives. A good shepherd would pick up a sheep and carry it on his back, if need be, to keep it safe, and that's what our shepherd will do for us!

God will meet your needs. Think back to the times in your life when worry and stress consumed you. When you trusted God, didn't He come through for you? If He hadn't, I doubt you'd be here today reading this book!

Remember to be grateful for all the times and all the ways God has provided for you so that you lack nothing you truly need. After all, He gave up His only Son to die on a cross for you—there's nothing He wouldn't do for you! Gratefulness for all He has done is a powerful antidote to worry.

"Do not be anxious about anything" *(Philippians 4:6).* Most of us take our cars to the dealership or a mechanic when a warning light turns on. When feelings of anxiety arise inside of you, don't try to fix the problem yourself! Instead, run to *your* Maker and turn the anxiety over to Him because He knows exactly what's wrong and how to fix it. Then, like Elijah, you can return to your life in the world and all of its challenges with the full assurance that God is with you and He is for you.

If the internal soundtrack to your life is anything like *Jaws*, it's time to change the music to Psalm 23. It's time to let those simple words of reassurance wash over you: "The LORD is my shepherd, I lack nothing" (Psalm 23:1).

WORKBOOK

Chapter One Questions

Question: God is present in your life, here and now. How have you seen Him personally involved in your life? How has God provided for you in the past? What is your understanding of the truth that you lack nothing?

_____

_____

_____

_____

_____

_____

_____

_____

_____

_____

Question: What concerns cause the most anxiety in your life? How can you surrender those anxieties to God?

_____

_____

_____

_____

_____

_____

_____

_____

_____

_____

Question: In what ways do you try to stay in control, and how can you release control to God instead?

_____

_____

_____

_____

_____

_____

_____

_____

_____

_____

_____

Question: How do you relate to God's personal name, Yahweh? Do you see Him as both sovereign and personal, or do you tend to lean toward one aspect more than the other?

_____

_____

_____

_____

_____

_____

_____

_____

_____

Action: There are several ways you can deal with your anxiety, including not facing your struggle alone. Think of one or two people in your life from whom you would like to seek counsel regularly. Ask them if they would be willing to be that resource for you when you are going through times of anxiety. Remember that God is always available for you. Like Elijah, take the time to unload your anxiety on God and give Him the opportunity to quiet your soul through His still, small voice.

Chapter One Notes

_____

_____

_____

_____

_____

_____

_____

_____

_____

_____

_____

_____

_____

_____

_____

_____

_____

_____

_____

_____

CHAPTER TWO

Following God's Lead

He makes me lie down in green pastures, he leads me beside quiet waters, he refreshes my soul. He guides me along the right paths for his name's sake.
—Psalm 23:2–3

Every year, I travel to the Amazon to lead a pastor's conference with a team from Justice and Mercy International. Many nights, I stand on the balcony of the center in the middle of the Amazon jungle, looking up at the stars, and I feel so small compared to how truly big God is. There's something about separating ourselves from all the distractions and cares of life that brings us an acute sense of God's presence and faithfulness.

We know from the previous chapter that God takes care of us like a shepherd cares for his sheep. But what does that look like? The rest of Psalm 23 gives us some insight into the practical ways God will care for us in life.

Notice that Psalm 23:2 says that God *makes* us lie down. He has to make us lie down because many times, we don't want to. We tend to think that we know best, and then we're off and running! We want to go our own way and do things our own way.

God knows what we need. He knows how our minds, bodies, and souls work. But once we get moving in a certain direction, we don't like to stop. We convince ourselves that we're making progress, even if we're running in the wrong direction!

Sometimes God has to slow us down for our own good. It can be painful and cause us to question our own faith. We may question the goodness of God, our shepherd. Sometimes the loss of a job, the end of a cherished relationship, or an illness can be God's way of making us lie down and truly value our lives. God knows what we need. He will take care of us and lead us to green pastures.

He makes us lie down in green pastures. David's kingdom contained a lot of barren, rocky wilderness, but a shepherd knew where to find the green pastures. The sheep didn't know where to find these pastures. Their tendency was to wander, which is our tendency, too.

In this psalm, "green pastures" refers to what is good for us, the good stuff that we truly need. The green pastures are what will nourish and refresh us: being in relationship with God, consuming His Word, worshiping His name, and living in His love. When we're in a place of doing these things, our worry, anxiety, and fear recede.

He leads us beside quiet waters. Our shepherd doesn't just point us in the right direction. He doesn't drive us forward by force, either. Instead, He goes ahead of us to lead us. Jesus said to His disciples, "Come, follow me" (Matthew 4:19).

He doesn't lead us to rushing waters, but to quiet waters. If we slip and fall in, we won't be swept away. These are waters that refresh us, calm us, and give us a presence of peace!

He refreshes our souls. Refreshment of the soul is what we need in the midst of anxiety, isn't it? After all, it is the soul that's either calm or distraught. The soul is where anxiety takes root. Places of refreshment, whether in our own quiet time with the Lord or in community with our church, are essential. If we don't build this kind of refreshment into our lives, life will leave us burned out and empty, with nothing left to give others.

He guides us along the right paths. God knows us better than we know ourselves, and He can see which way is the right way, the "right path," for each of us. That means we *can* trust God and His leading; the question is whether we *do* trust Him.

It is for His name's sake. This phrase—"for His name's sake"—is another way of saying "for God's glory." Because we are God's sheep, we represent and reflect Him, our shepherd, while we travel the path He has laid out for us. After all, *Christian* means a follower of Jesus, the Christ! He is leading us to become more like Him.

Why Are We Anxious?

God is at work in each of our lives and knows where we need to go. He is our shepherd, ready to lead us along the right path. So, why do we get anxious?

The average adult makes 35,000 decisions a day, and our children are facing 3,000 decisions a day.[5] When you turn on Netflix, you have to make what seems like a thousand decisions. Getting dressed in the morning, you may take twenty minutes just to decide which outfit to wear. Making a sandwich, you may be deciding among turkey, ham, and roast beef. Have you ever been to the chip aisle at the grocery store? It's crazy! It's overwhelming, right? There's more anxiety in America than in third-world countries,[6] and I think it's because we're faced with making so many choices.

I don't think God cares about what kind of sandwich you eat, but we all have big decisions to make in our lives, such as whom to date, which job to take, and how to discipline our children. God cares about these things! You have a choice to make in all of this: will you trust God?

Remember, a little anxiety is sometimes healthy. It may mean that God is leading us in a certain way, such as to get off the couch and read His Word, go to church, or look for a job. God will lead us, but we must choose to follow.

A little bit of fear can charge us up, but excessive worry, anxiety, or fear is unhealthy. It can function like a check-engine light, warning us that we need to deal with something. Excessive worry may mean that we need more downtime so our souls can be refreshed. Existing in this constant preemptive state of anxiety is not what God wants for us.

Fighting the Pandemic of Anxiety

In the Old Testament, Joshua was Moses' right-hand guy. In the opening chapter of Joshua, God called Joshua to lead His people after Moses died. Forty years earlier, the people wouldn't follow Moses into the Promised Land, so I'm sure you can imagine how intimidating it was for Joshua to be given the task. I'm sure that he had a lot of worry in the face of leading a million people!

It makes me think about how my dad went home to be with the Lord five years ago. I miss him, and there are still times in my life when I wonder what my dad would have done if faced with various challenges. I'm sure that Joshua had the same thought: "What would Moses do?" These were the moments when Joshua was called to trust God. In Joshua 1:9, the Bible says, "Have I not commanded you? Be strong and courageous. Do not be afraid; do not be discouraged, for the LORD your God will be with you wherever you go."

God can give you courage in the chaos, as He did for Joshua. You can be a strong Christian and still deal with worry, anxiety, and fear. It's okay, but it's not okay to stay there. When you give God your heart, you have every tool to deal with the pandemic of worry, anxiety, and fear.

Start with Prayer

An article in the *Wall Street Journal* said that men tend to express anxiety differently from women, usually through anger or alcohol consumption.[7] This will eat you alive! It's surprising how often we'll try to solve problems ourselves or turn to things like alcohol or "retail therapy" before we pray about them.

In Luke 9:23, Jesus said to His disciples, "Whoever wants to be my disciple must deny themselves and take up their cross daily and follow me." Jesus followed His own advice. He went off by Himself, pulling away from everyone to be with His Father. It would make sense that this would be necessary for us as well.

It may seem difficult to make time to be alone with God, especially in a culture where loneliness is an epidemic. But there's so much noise in this world, and it's imperative that we prioritize spending time with God. It's easy to start reading our Bible and then get distracted by our phones and scrolling through Instagram. I think that's why God established the Sabbath in the Ten Commandments.

Planning a Sabbath is one way to make time to hear God. In times like this, His still, small voice will lead you. We all need to get away from the noise and take time to listen. Worship, church, and hearing God's Word make for a healthy Sabbath.

It's also important to build margins into our lives. We live overscheduled and overcrowded lives. We need boundaries to protect our time and emotional health. Physician and author Richard Swenson, M.D., describes *margin* this way: "Margin is the space between our load and our limits. It is the amount beyond that which is needed. It is something held in reserve for contingencies or unanticipated situations. Margin is the gap between rest and exhaustion, the space between breathing freely and suffocating."[8] Margins in our lives allow us to remain healthy.

We take time to work out physically and stay sharp mentally, but what about our souls? Jesus said, "What good is it for someone to gain the whole world, yet forfeit their soul?" (Mark 8:36). We are after money and success, but is it enough? Learning to be content with our time and resources is essential. Our call, as His sheep, is to follow God and nourish our souls in Him.

Trust God's Plans

Worry, fear, and anxiety come because we think we know more than God knows. However, God's plans are better than ours. Perspective is everything. Even when it doesn't seem to be going our way, God has something bigger and better. One door may close, but God will open a new one! God's plans are better than our plans.

Like Joshua, we will still face challenges. Joshua still had to walk around Jericho, face the giants in the land, and fight some big battles, but God was with him. Joshua could have stayed in the desert and avoided these challenges, but he knew that God had so much more.

If you stare at a problem long enough, it grows bigger. When you start to focus on God, that problem starts to look different. He is always doing something bigger in your life than what you can see. Trusting God's calling in your life and His ability to see it through is an important part of overcoming anxiety in your life.

A Matter of Obedience

The most anxious time of my life was when God called me and my wife, Lisa, to plant a new church, Rolling Hills. I had a good job at the time, with great benefits. Then I started hearing God say, "I want you to start a new church." I initially resisted this call. However, the more I investigated the idea, the more I heard that still, small voice calling me to plant a church.

Someone approached me one day and asked, "How are you going to support a family?" I honestly hadn't thought about it, so I didn't know.

A pivotal moment was when I heard the Holy Spirit's voice: "Are you going to trust Me or not?" I couldn't ignore the call any longer. Even though we didn't have the answers to all our questions, ultimately it became a matter of prioritizing obedience, faith, and trust over anxiety.

After moving, my wife and I started a Bible study with fifteen people in an apartment clubhouse on Thursday nights. With such a small start, I wondered if I was crazy. The day after the first Bible study, while I was walking alongside a river, a verse came to my mind:

Do not be anxious about anything, but in every situation, by prayer and petition, with thanksgiving, present your requests to God. And the peace of God, which transcends all

understanding, will guard your hearts and your minds in Christ Jesus.
                                        —Philippians 4:6–7

I must have quoted that verse a hundred times alongside that river. I didn't have all the answers, but I knew that I'd rather be with God and trust Him than just stay in my current job. Peace truly did fill my soul!

When I trusted God, He freed me. I look back now and think, "God, why didn't I trust You more?" When you are outside of God's will, there will naturally be tension in your life.

Take your thirty thousand decisions and boil them down to one: will I trust Him? Decide that He is enough for you and that you will follow Him. He is. Make this one decision every day—to hold your life with open hands, trusting God—and He will lead you where you need to be.

The Quakers pray with their hands open. They are essentially saying, "God, I am all Yours. I have open hands and a heart open to Your will." Like the Quakers, open your hands and your heart to God. Even if you don't understand everything, ask God to show Himself to you and reveal His will. When He does, follow. It will be better than you can imagine!

Chapter Two Questions

Question: Has God ever used circumstances to make you lie down? In what ways did He bring refreshment through those times in ways you didn't expect?

_____

_____

_____

_____

_____

_____

_____

_____

_____

_____

_____

Question: How can you prioritize taking time to refresh your soul so that you don't burn out in your own strength?

_____

_____

_____

_____

_____

_____

_____

_____

_____

_____

Question: Is there any excessive worry in your life acting as a warning light? What do you think it's pointing to that you may need to deal with?

_____

_____

_____

_____

_____

_____

_____

_____

_____

_____

_____

_____

Question: Is anxiety keeping you from obedience? What is He calling you to do? Do you trust God to lead you?

_____

_____

_____

_____

_____

_____

_____

_____

_____

_____

_____

Question: If you stare at a problem long enough, it grows bigger. What problems are you staring at? How can you begin to focus on God instead?

_____

_____

_____

_____

_____

_____

_____

_____

_____

_____

_____

Question: Do you practice the Sabbath in your weekly routine to bring your focus back to resting in God? How can you take time to be with your Father like Jesus did?

_____

_____

_____

_____

_____

_____

_____

_____

_____

_____

_____

Action: Meditate on Philippians 4:6–7 this week and take time to memorize it. Whenever worry arises, recite the verse to yourself.

Chapter Two Notes

CHAPTER THREE

Walking Through the Valley

Even though I walk through the darkest valley....
—Psalm 23:4a

"Why? Why is this happening to me?" is a question that most people ask at some point in their lives. Do you remember the first time you asked this question? That place of despair is a spiritual valley that we will all walk through at some point in our lives.

Maybe anxiety has been your biggest challenge. For some people, it's a lifelong struggle. Even when you understand the keys to overcoming anxiety, fear, worry, and stress, you still have to learn to put those keys into practice when you encounter difficult situations or seasons. Spiritual valleys are not enjoyable to walk through, but they also have the potential to strengthen your faith like never before.

Through the Valley

In Psalm 23:4, after talking about how God cares for us, King David takes a sharp turn and begins talking about "the darkest valley." Because he himself had been a shepherd, David understood that shepherds had to lead their flocks from meadow to meadow in hilly or mountainous terrain. For example, depending on the season, they might have to go from lowland meadows to highland meadows or vice versa. Traveling between meadows in search of a better meadow required passing through valleys, which often weren't great places to be. They had deep ravines, dangerous predators, unstable ground, and potential for flooding. But a good shepherd led his sheep through the valleys.

It's important to realize that God, as our shepherd, leads us through valleys, not around them. We see this truth played out time and again in Scripture.

The Christian's Suffering

James, the half-brother of Jesus who wrote the book of James, didn't follow Jesus during His earthly ministry. It's possible that James thought Jesus was crazy when He started talking about being the Messiah. What made James believe that his brother was the Son of God?

The resurrection of Jesus from the dead was what changed his mind. Think about what it would take for your own brother to convince you that he is the Messiah. James put his own life on the line. Then he joined the rest of the disciples. Jesus had told the disciples not to go out and share the gospel with the rest of the world until the Holy Spirit came upon them. Acts 2 describes how the Spirit came to the disciples at Pentecost, after which Peter stood up and delivered a sermon. That's when the church was born in Jerusalem, and thousands came to know Christ.

But the Roman government and the Pharisees didn't like this much and began persecuting the followers of Jesus. In response to the persecution and suffering of the early church, James wrote the book of James as a letter that still holds significance for us today.

It is worth noting that after James wrote the letter, he was beheaded by King Herod for his faith (Acts 12:2). In the second verse of his letter, James wrote, "Consider it pure joy, my brothers and sisters, whenever you face trials of many kinds" (James 1:2). The people in the early church were suffering because of their decision to follow Jesus.

Your suffering may look different from theirs, but in the early church, as well as now, many people have responded to suffering by wondering, "Why is God letting this happen?" Why doesn't God eliminate suffering? The fact that God allows people to suffer, including people who love Him and follow Jesus, can seem troubling to believers. Non-believers often point to the "problem of suffering" as justification for not believing in God or following Jesus.

But would a good God eliminate suffering? When we think that God should get rid of our difficulties, it's like we want an indulgent grandfather in heaven instead of a Father in heaven. Grandparents often like to spoil their grandchildren, which can be at odds with the discipline and lessons that parents try to instill in their children. C. S. Lewis noted that when we really love someone, we would rather "see them suffer much than be happy in contempt-ible and estranging modes." [9]

We live in a fallen, broken world. Because of sin, there are struggles in this life. One day, Jesus will make all things right, but until then, we will all walk through hurt and brokenness. There is pain, suffering, and even death.

Pain can help us to grow. We can't get rid of pain; it's unavoidable. We can't snap our fingers and make it all go away. What matters isn't eliminating pain from our lives but responding to it in the right way. What will you choose to do with your pain?

Purpose in the Valleys

When I go through tough times, I'm not usually think-ing about joy. You may wonder whether James understood what "joy" means! What about finding joy in puppies, laughing babies, or walks on the beach in 72-de-gree weather, instead? Those seem a lot more joyful than crisis, illness, or the loss of a job.

Some people in the early church might have been con-fused at what James wrote. However, James wasn't addressing the faint of heart. He also wasn't saying to be joyful *about* their difficult circumstances; he said to be joyful *in* them.

Joy doesn't mean happiness. Happiness is based on cir-cumstances. When things are good, we are happy. When things are bad or tough, we are not happy. Joy, on the other hand, is based on Christ, and Christ does not change.

He "is the same yesterday and today and forever" (Hebrews 13:8). This is how we can be joyful despite our circumstances and in all circumstances. If we are depending on God, we can "rejoice always" (1 Thessalonians 5:16–18).

Joy is deeper and more enduring than happiness. David speaks of this joy in Psalm 4:7: "You have filled my heart with greater joy than when their grain and new wine abound" (NIV84). Two kinds of joy are contrasted here: inward joy, which comes from knowing and trusting God, and happiness, which comes as a result of pleasant circumstances. Inward joy is steady, as long as we trust God, while happiness is unpredictable. Inward joy defeats discouragement, but happiness covers it up. Happiness is temporary, but inward joy can last forever.[10]

There is a level of holiness that comes with our pain because difficult times lead us to become more dependent on God, like sheep depend on the shepherd to lead them through the dark valley. The valleys of life make us more attentive to our shepherd. We draw closer to Him because we know that if we veer away from Him, predators are lurking.

There is purpose in these valleys. Paul wrote in his letter to the Romans:

> And we boast in the hope of the glory of God. Not only so, but we also glory in our sufferings, because we know that suffering produces perseverance; perseverance, character; and character, hope. And hope does not put us to shame, because God's love has been poured out into our hearts through the Holy Spirit, who has been given to us.
> —*Romans 5:2b–5*

Are you having difficulty understanding or coming to terms with your suffering? James wrote that you should ask God for wisdom: "If any of you lacks wisdom, you should ask God, who gives generously to all without finding fault, and it will be given to you" (James 1:5). Wisdom leads to understanding our purpose.

The early church understood suffering. They often had to leave their homes, their friends, their families, and the lives they knew for the cause of Christ. They probably wondered where their next meal would come from and how they would feed their children. Some days, they probably couldn't. But their purpose was greater than their difficulty. They were trusting Jesus and His promise of eternal life.

Our pain is meaningless in this world until we find purpose in it. If the shepherd doesn't lead the sheep through the valley, they will miss out on the opportunity for greater nourishment available on the other side of it. God allows and leads us through the valleys to deepen our faith and trust in Him and our dependence on Him. When we come to the other side and discover that He never left us and encounter the spacious place He has led us into, we understand the purpose of the valley.

Also, the valleys can lead us deeper into our relationship with our shepherd. Often when we are going through a valley, we want to get through it quickly. But what if, in the midst of the valley, we ask God what He is trying to teach us? How do we grow stronger in our love for Him and for others? Sometimes it is in the valley that God does the best work in our lives.

Chapter Three Questions

Question: How has God met you in your greatest spiritual valleys? How has He used despair to strengthen your faith?

_____

_____

_____

_____

_____

_____

_____

_____

_____

_____

Question: As you look back on your life, can you think of times when God has met you in a valley and brought you through it?

_____

_____

_____

_____

_____

_____

_____

_____

_____

_____

Question: What is joy? How can you be joyful in the middle of difficult circumstances?

_____

_____

_____

_____

_____

_____

_____

_____

_____

_____

_____

Question: Do you know people who have used their pain to bring glory to God? What can you learn from their example?

_____

_____

_____

_____

_____

_____

_____

_____

_____

_____

_____

Action: Think of one practical way you can use your pain to bring glory to God this week, and then put that plan into practice. For example, if your pain is loneliness, maybe you can turn that into empathy for someone else who has a similar struggle and reach out to that person to share God's love.

Chapter Three Notes

CHAPTER FOUR

Calm in the Storm

I will fear no evil, for you are with me; your rod and your staff, they comfort me.

—Psalm 23:4b

If you want to know about stress, then just teach your daughter to drive! This will take you to a whole different level of stress. There's no brake on the passenger side, and no matter how hard you press your foot to the floorboard, it doesn't stop the car.

I'm stressed and worried about letting her out on the road because I don't trust anyone else out there to care for her the way I do. I want to put bubble wrap all over the car, put one of those safety signs on it, and tell everyone to stay away, because she's my baby girl and I want her to be safe.

There are all sorts of things to worry about in your life. For example, have you ever had symptoms of various kinds and then searched on the Internet trying to self-diagnose your issue? In the process, did you find out that you *must* have terminal cancer? Opportunities to worry are all around us. God calls us to "be anxious for nothing" (Philippians 4:6 NKJV), but we don't know how. There are so many things for us to fret over!

The world tries to sell us a cheap imitation of peace. The world tells us that if we make enough money, we'll have no more worries. But it doesn't really work; it doesn't address the root of our fears. Jennifer Aniston said in a *New York Times* article that there are days when she just wants to cry,[11] and even Justin Bieber has said that there are days when it's hard for him to get out of bed.[12] They have so much money, and even they battle anxiety! In the words of Richard Watts, a financial and legal advisor to the very rich, "There's some truth to the saying, 'more money, more problems.'"[13]

We live in a world of fear and evil—pandemics, mass shootings, human trafficking, abuse, and pornography, to name some of the brokenness that surrounds us. This is not how God created the world to be. God created a perfect world filled with good things; everything was perfect. Man was in perfect relationship with God and all creation.

Then sin entered the world, and everything changed. Although worry, anxiety, and fear are at an all-time high today, we are not designed to be consumed by them. God said that in this world, we can still have peace. He didn't give up on the world at the time of the fall of man, and He doesn't give up on us today. There is evil in this world, but God makes hope, peace, and comfort available if we want them.

God with Us

David said in Psalm 23:4, "I will fear no evil...." We live in a fallen world, and David recognized this. There is evil. So, how can we have no fear? When you read on, the answer lies in the text: "...for you are with me" (Psalm 23:4).

In the incarnation, we find a God who truly is with us. It is written in John 1:14, "And the Word became flesh and dwelt among us" (NKJV). Jesus came into a world that was evil. The Romans were experts at killing people, slavery was rampant, orgies were normal, and debauchery was everywhere.

Even in the midst of this, everyone was looking for peace. The theme of Roman rule would become *Pax Romana*, "the peace of Rome," but Rome brought anything but peace. However, Jesus came in the midst of chaos to reveal His *true* peace.

Jesus doesn't take us out of the world, but He is with us in the world. He came to walk among us in order to restore peace. He triumphed over evil on the cross for us! God takes us through the greenest pasture and the darkest valley. He is with us through it all, and we can have peace in it all.

Peace with God comes not in the absence of storms, but in the presence of Jesus. In John 16:33, Jesus said, "I have told you these things, so that in me you may have peace. In this world you will have trouble. But take heart! I have overcome the world." Jesus is how we overcome anxiety, worry, and fear in our lives today. In one sovereign act, Jesus overcame it all. We must live in the assurance of His promise, even in the midst of the storms of this life.

In Mark 4, there was a storm. We're talking *massive* waves. Experienced fishermen were in the boat, and Jesus was asleep on a cushion in the stern. The disciples woke Jesus and asked, "Teacher, don't you care if we drown?" (Mark 4:38). Jesus got up and rebuked the wind and the waves. The wind died down, and it was calm. He asked the disciples why they were so afraid. Why are *you* afraid?

Jesus still calms storms today. Whatever storm you're facing today, remember Jesus. Don't forget about Him! Peace doesn't come in the absence of storms. Peace comes in the presence of Jesus.

Jesus, Our Peace

We all long for peace, and many times we try to manufacture peace through vacations or spa days. We often say that we want "a moment's peace," but we need more than a moment. We need a lifetime of peace, and only Jesus can supply it. A moment's peace only leaves us wanting more.

David, as a shepherd, understood the importance of the rod and the staff, two essentials for shepherding. Therefore, in Psalm 23:4, he acknowledges the peace and comfort that come with knowing that Jesus is with us, carrying both rod and staff: "I will fear no evil, for you are with me; your rod and your staff, they comfort me."

A shepherd's rod, a club generally three feet long with pieces of flint and metal driven into the end of it, was most often his weapon to fight off wild animals and thieves.

The shepherd's staff, often six feet long and hooked on one end, was helpful for maintaining sure footing and for knocking down foliage for food. The shepherd also used his staff to guide the sheep and help them to navigate rough terrain. If a sheep fell into a ditch, got stuck in the brush, or fell into deep or swift-moving water, the shepherd would use his staff to rescue the creature. Every night, the shepherd stood with his staff as all of the sheep passed by, and he counted them and inspected each one for injury and illness.[14]

The rod and the staff are two different symbols of Jesus, our protector and rescuer. Jesus is our peace! We think that when we get past something—a test, a job interview, a financial crisis—we will have peace. However, there's always something else. The pace of our lives keeps us always searching for the next pocket of peace. But peace isn't found in circumstances; it's found in God alone, our shepherd.

In a Hurry

We're often in a hurry, allowing fear and anxiety to rule over us. My good friend Amy Alexander is the cofounder and executive director of The Refuge Center for Counseling. She said, "The pace of life brings anxiety." She pointed out that we aren't pausing often enough in the course of our days and weeks to let us grow as people. Instead, "we are just trying to produce more."

Jesus was never in a hurry, yet He changed the world. Jesus had a right relationship with God, others, and

Himself. Today, Jesus is able to calm the hurry in our lives like He calmed the wind in Matthew 14.

When Peter "saw the wind," he began to sink (Matthew 14:30). The wind isn't something you can see, so what was he seeing that made him so afraid? We also have the propensity to worry about things that never happen. We compare ourselves to others and have a fear of missing out, thinking that we are being left behind.

Peter was afraid, and what did Jesus do? He took Peter's hand and pulled him up. Paul David Tripp writes, "If all Jesus wants to do is relieve the difficulty, He wouldn't have to take the walk. All He would need to do is say a prayer from the shore and the wind would cease. He takes the walk because He is not after the difficulty. He is after the men in the middle of the difficulty."[15]

Jesus overcame the world, including all the storms in it. *He* is how we find peace when anxiety, worry, and fear bombard us.

The Presence of Jesus

Peter wasn't perfect. You'd think that after everything he witnessed Jesus do firsthand, his faith would have been through the roof. But when a storm—the arrest of Jesus—came into his life again, Peter denied Jesus three times (Matthew 26:69–75). Then, after the resurrection, he went back to his old life as a fisherman (John 21:1–3). At this point, I'm sure he was filled with shame and guilt. But Jesus showed up (John 21:4) and rescued him yet again. God wasn't finished with Peter.

It is written in 1 Peter 5:7, "Cast all your anxiety on him because he cares for you." I am sure that when Peter wrote this, he thought of the very day when Jesus reached out to him in the midst of the storm. Peter was afraid in the storm, but he grew to become a person of great faith.

God doesn't want us to live in fear. He wants us to live in faith. As the Bible says in Romans 8:31, "If God is for us, who can be against us?" In the midst of whatever you face, focus on Jesus. Jesus said, "Peace I leave with you; my peace I give you. I do not give to you as the world gives. Do not let your hearts be troubled and do not be afraid" (John 14:27). He has given you His peace.

Be Still

My friend Amy also said, "Anxiety is actually a cue. This is actually something that God designed into our bodies! God created the vagus nerve and the amygdala to send us messages. Physiologically, anxiety is actually just a messenger. When it comes up, we need to listen to the message."

My friend Pike, who also works at The Refuge Center and is a licensed therapist, said, "Embrace the idea that you're actually afraid. We don't allow a lot of space for emotions, so we're not comfortable acknowledging our emotions. It's okay to be afraid."

Sometimes we're scared to get up close and personal with our fears and consider what the root cause of our anxiety is. The Bible clearly states in Psalm 46:10, "Be still, and know that I am God." A lot of people don't want to be still because then they'll have to be honest with themselves and with God. It's easier to keep busy instead of doing the hard work to get healthy. When we get still with God and are honest about our fears and anxieties, we can surrender them to Him. Being vulnerable in the stillness of God's presence is where we find peace.

With Us Through It All

You're not alone. God is there, and He is for you! Jesus brings us peace with God, peace with others, and peace with ourselves. God has our eternal life secure. He is enough for us.

In this world, we live with so much anxiety, worry, and fear, yet we must remember that God is with us through it all. Our tendency is to look at the wind and the waves around us, to focus on our problems and struggles.

However, when we look up, Jesus is there with His arms outstretched to us. Will you take His hand? Will you receive His grace and peace in your life? Whatever you are facing, know that Jesus is greater. He still calms the storms and redeems lives. God is with you and for you.

WORKBOOK

Chapter Four Questions

Question: How has God given you peace in the midst of life's storms? God is the One who calms the storms. How can you remember this in your daily life?

_____

_____

_____

_____

_____

_____

_____

_____

_____

_____

Question: Peace comes in the presence of Jesus. In what ways can you live your life in His presence and experience His peace?

_____

_____

_____

_____

_____

_____

_____

_____

_____

_____

_____

Question: What are you worried about that may never happen? How can you surrender these worries to God?

_____

_____

_____

_____

_____

_____

_____

_____

_____

_____

_____

_____

Action: Acknowledge your feelings (fear, anxiety, worry, etc.) and invite God into them. Take time to be vulnerable in the stillness of God's presence so that He can expose the root of these feelings.

Chapter Four Notes

CHAPTER FIVE

Save Your Fork!

You prepare a table before me in the presence of my ene-mies. You anoint my head with oil; my cup overflows.
—Psalm 23:5

When I was growing up, one of my favorite holidays was Thanksgiving. Every Thanksgiving, we would go visit my grandmother. My grandma's cooking was off the charts!

On Thanksgiving, she would prepare a feast—turkey, ham, and sometimes even fried chicken (because that's what you do in West Texas). We would eat this wonderful meal, laugh, and talk. Then my grandma would say the three most incredible words: "Save your fork!" We knew what that meant. We knew that even though the food was really good, the best was yet to come. Grandma could bake some amazing pies, cobbler, and cake. We saved our forks to eat these delights.

God is working in our lives both now and in the not-yet. There is a banquet being prepared. He will take care of you and bless you now, but save your fork because the best is yet to come! We live in this world, and He gives us access to His peace, but He is also saying, "You just wait! It's going to get better! Trust Me."

God's Blessing

In Psalm 23:5, there's a shift. We move from God being our *shepherd* to God being our *host*. Did you notice something else in this verse? You don't prepare the table. God does! God is the host, and He prepares a table for you. He makes it personal.

Not only is this very personal, but He also prepares a table in the presence of your enemies. Jesus said, "The thief comes only to steal and kill and destroy" (John 10:10a). That's what Satan wants to do in all of our lives. He wants to steal our joy, kill our relationships, and bring death to our lives. Our enemies are excessive anxiety, worry, and fear that steal our joy and keep us from being present in our lives. They rob us of the life that God wants for us. Jesus said, "I have come that they may have life, and have it to the full" (John 10:10b).

God prepares a table for you, and He also anoints you and gives you an overflowing cup. The anointing of oil was the customary treatment for an honored guest. And there isn't just a little bit of goodness—it's overflowing! God spoils you.

We are on the winning team, and God is calling us not to be anxious about anything. God not only protects and rescues us, as symbolized by the rod and the staff, but He also blesses us, granting us mercy and grace.

Mercy is when we don't get what we deserve. For example, say that you're driving along, and the speed limit is 35 miles per hour, but you're going 46 miles per hour. You're over the speed limit, and when you see the lights behind you, you fill up with dread. You pull over to the side. The police officer comes up and says, "Excuse me. Do you know that you were going over the speed limit?" After a short exchange, the police officer says, "I'm just going to give you a warning." You are relieved because you know that you deserve a ticket, but you get mercy.

We all know that we deserve death because of our sin. However, God, in His mercy, sent His Son to pay the price for us!

In addition to mercy, with God, there is also grace. Grace is when we get what we don't deserve. What if the police officer came up and said, "Hey, not only am I going to give you just a warning, but I'm also going to pay off your car"? It would be unbelievable! But that's a small glimpse of what God has done for us.

God gives us a home, food, and clothes. God gives us a community. He gives us things that we don't deserve. He gives us the gift of the Holy Spirit. He gives us Himself!

In 1 John 3:1, the Bible says, "See what great love the Father has lavished on us, that we should be called children of God! And that is what we are!" Think about all the blessings we have in God—His great love, presence, protection, and provision. We have been given so much!

Gratitude and Giving

Two of the greatest antidotes to anxiety, worry, and fear are gratitude and giving. As a nation, we chose a day to stop and focus on being thankful and generous. Every day should be Thanksgiving when we are in Christ Jesus!

So often we get discouraged because we spend our time comparing ourselves to others whom we see as better off than we are. We're on social media being filled with anxiety, worry, and fear because we feel that we are missing out on something. But what if we were to stop comparing ourselves to others? What if we were to spend our time thinking about all we have in Christ—joy, peace, the presence of God in our lives, forgiveness, love, and eternal life to come? Are you thankful for what He has provided? He has lavished so much on us!

Robert J. Morgan summed up much of what we have in Christ: "If you are carrying around emotional baggage, damaged emotions, hurtful memories, and unresolved shame, you'll find blessed freedom at the foot of the cross. And when you are justified, you have peace with God, access to grace, assurance of heaven, redemption from suffering, the Holy Spirit and his love, freedom from the coming day of wrath—and you have Jesus Christ Himself. Hallelujah!"[16]

We have been given so much, but God's Word says, "It is more blessed to give than to receive" (Acts 20:35). When we give, it releases something inside of us. We are most like God when we give. We can't outgive Him! When we give, our lives are transformed.

Generosity in Action

There's a ministry in Nashville called The Bridge that makes living generously its priority. They work with over five hundred homeless people, feeding them and holding a worship service night every week under a bridge in downtown Nashville. They also feed over four thousand kids every day.

The founder of The Bridge is Candy Christmas. Fifteen years ago, Candy was a very successful worship artist performing gospel music all over the world, but she started going through depression. She said that she didn't even want to leave her house.

One day, there was a man at her friend's house laying tile. He told her, "Lady, you look like you need a little pick-me-up. You look like you haven't eaten in a while." He proceeded to tell her that he and a few people fed the homeless downtown, and if she came, she could also get a meal.

She didn't need the meal, but she decided to join him. She made a big pot of jambalaya and drove downtown to feed the homeless. She ended up going the following week and every week after that. Then she started telling her family and friends about the ministry, and they began bringing food. After a few weeks, her entire garage was filled with food.

After seven weeks, her husband said, "Candy, you're not depressed anymore!" She told him, "I didn't even think about it!" Now they have nine full-time staff at The Bridge, and Candy has found so much joy through giving to others.

God blesses us, but it's not just for us. He blesses us so we can be a blessing. And then we can invite others to sit at the table. It's amazing how giving and serving will change your life. Joy truly comes in giving.

Setting the Table for Others

Now that the table has been set for us, we are called to set the table for others, to be the hands and feet of Jesus in order to bless those around us. We've been blessed to be a blessing! In Luke 6:38, it is written, "Give, and it will be given to you. A good measure, pressed down, shaken together and running over, will be poured into your lap. For with the measure you use, it will be measured to you." When you give, there is a joy that's released in you.

The church I have the privilege of serving learned this lesson early on. Eighteen years ago, we started a Bible study of fifteen people. We knew that it couldn't just be about us, so we decided to take a mission trip. Eight months later, eighteen of us went to Moldova. We didn't even know where Moldova was initially, but we'd heard about the need that was there in the poorest country in the former Soviet Union.

We went to Moldova to serve the less fortunate, yet God ended up changing *our* lives through the experience! We fell in love with the people and went back again the next year to minister to orphans. We made the trip again the following year.

After a couple of years, we saw a need with orphans who graduate out of the system at fifteen or sixteen but have no place to go. We decided that we should start a nonprofit to buy houses for these kids to have a safe place to live. As a church, we didn't have our own property in the United States, but we built a $250,000 home in Moldova for orphans and vulnerable children as a transitional home for those who have no place to go. Today we have four houses in Moldova through Justice and Mercy International and are planning to build two more.

When talking about missions, you may have anxiety, stress, worry, and fear. You may think, "I can't go to Moldova. No way! I can't give money to sponsor a child. I don't have that much money! I can't serve at church. I don't have time!"

God doesn't want you to have a scarcity mentality. He wants you to look at Him! He is the One who pours your cup to overflowing.

Here's what happens when you give and serve: your life is the one that is changed. You can't live the same way. You are given a greater awareness of God's grace, love, and perspective.

God invited us to the table, and now we are called to set the table for others. The Bible says in James 1:27, "Religion that God our Father accepts as pure and faultless is this: to look after orphans and widows in their distress and to keep oneself from being polluted by the world." When stress, worry, fear, and anxiety come, do something for someone else.

We have all been blessed not just for us, but for us to be a blessing to others. When we think about all that God has done for us, we quickly see our anxiety subside. When we realize that God is sovereign over all creation and He is the One who is with us, then we are able to give and invest in others. We experience joy as we become the hands and feet of Christ. God is the greatest Giver of all—He gave His one and only Son for us! In the same way, we are most like God when we love and when we give.

God wants us to live every day like it's Thanksgiving. He wants us to be grateful. When we live with the knowledge that we have a God who loves us, we can extend that love generously to others.

WORKBOOK

Chapter Five Questions

Question: In what ways has the enemy stolen, killed, and brought destruction in your life? How have you seen God redeem these offenses through preparing a table before your enemy?

_____

_____

_____

_____

_____

_____

_____

_____

_____

_____

Question: How has God revealed His grace and mercy in your life?

_____

_____

_____

_____

_____

_____

_____

_____

_____

_____

Question: Do you have a scarcity mentality? In what ways do you see God pouring out His blessings on your life? How have you seen God change your life when you have served others?

_____

_____

_____

_____

_____

_____

_____

_____

_____

_____

Action: Practice thankfulness today. Take some time to write down things for which you are thankful. What is a way you can turn that thankfulness into generosity for others?

Chapter Five Notes

CHAPTER SIX

The Secret to Contentment

Surely your goodness and love will follow me all the days of my life, and I will dwell in the house of the LORD forever.
—Psalm 23:6

One year, we took our kids to Orlando on a family vacation. On one of the days, we visited Universal Studios. When we arrived, my middle daughter wanted to ride the Hulk roller coaster, which has seventy-seven inversions and goes sixty-six miles per hour. I said, "Let's do it!" Everyone else told us, "See you later!"

As we stood in line, listening to everyone scream, my daughter Mabry, who was twelve at the time, said, "Nope! Dad, I don't want to do it!" But I convinced her to stay. Every few minutes, she said that she didn't want to do it, and I would again convince her to stay in line with me. As we got closer, tears started rolling down her cheeks. After standing in line for so long and hearing her say this, I wondered if I should let her out of it, but I told her that the experience would be worth it.

Finally, we got on the ride and held hands tightly. The roller coaster shot off, and it was intense! I heard her screaming. I was holding on to her and to the bar in front of me as we flew up and down. When the ride finally ended, I asked her what she thought. She said, "That was awesome, Dad! It was so cool and so fun! Let's do it again!"

Life is like a roller coaster: there are many ups and downs, twists and turns. You don't know what to expect. My daughter had all of this anxiety and worry leading up to the roller coaster, but when she got on it, she thought it was awesome.

If you look back at your life, you may remember times of worry, but you can also remember that once you got through it, it all worked out. It has been said that we are all either in a crisis, coming out of a crisis, or going into a crisis. However, God is always faithful. He is the One we hold on to during this roller coaster we call life.

We live in a culture of anxiety, worry, and fear, but we don't have to give in to it. God doesn't want us to live with excessive anxiety, worry, and fear. God wants us to enjoy life and experience it to the fullest.

With You and for You

As a country, we live with a powerful enemy called anxiety. This is nothing new. People throughout time have dealt with this struggle, but the scale and impact on our lives is greater than ever before. Seventy-seven percent of people say that they are more anxious today than they

were one year ago.[17] This is not healthy, and we must stop
this trend.

We don't know what the future holds, but we know
who holds the future. God created us to enjoy life! We are
in the world but not of the world. May we truly learn to
"be anxious for nothing" (Philippians 4:6 NKJV).

I lead a biblical studies tour to Israel every few years
with a group from my church. It's incredible to be where
Jesus walked and to see the Bible come to life. When I go
to the Middle East, I see shepherds leading their sheep.
This is different from how shepherds control their flocks
in the United States. They tend to drive their sheep by
pushing from behind, but shepherds in the Middle East
lead their sheep.[18] David was a shepherd who led his
sheep. He knew them by name. He also had sheepdogs
who helped to protect his sheep. God also has sheepdogs—they are goodness and love.

A. W. Tozer said, "What comes into our minds when
we think about God is the most important thing about
us."[19] You may think that God has only judgment and condemnation for you. If you believe that God just wants to
punish you, then you will live with guilt and shame. But
in Romans 8:1, the Bible says, "Therefore, there is now
no condemnation for those who are in Christ Jesus." You
can know this God of goodness and love. Jesus changes
everything.

God is with you and for you. God isn't angry with you.
He wants the best for you, and He proved it by sending
Jesus to provide you with eternal life (John 3:16).

Think about this: you "will dwell in the house of the
LORD forever" (Psalm 23:6)! David knew that this life

isn't all there is. This is just the introduction. The best is still to come! In light of eternity, you can make it through anything, knowing that it's temporary.

This world isn't all there is, but it is our temporary home. We know that God will make all things right in the end: "For our light and momentary troubles are achieving for us an eternal glory that far outweighs them all" (2 Corinthians 4:17). Things may not seem light at the moment, but when you look at your life in the scope of eternity, you realize that God is with you and will make everything right. You can trust the One who holds your heart and has everything under His perfect control.

Control Versus Contentment

So much of our anxiety stems from control. We want to be in control, and when we are not, we become anxious, stressed, worried, and afraid. We really don't have as much control as we think we have. Our main job when it comes to control is to manage our attitude and response to a situation instead of trying to control the situation itself. Just like on a roller coaster, there are ups and downs in life, but God is with us through it all. He is leading and guiding us into something greater.

There are many things to worry about in life, things that we can't control. We try to protect our kids, but they grow up. We try to control our finances, but sometimes unexpected expenses come up. The stock market goes up, but it also comes down. We try to control our time, but we can't get any more hours in a day. The list goes on.

Jesus invites us not to worry and, instead, to enjoy the ride with Him:

> *Therefore I tell you, do not worry about your life, what you will eat or drink; or about your body, what you will wear. Is not life more than food, and the body more than clothes? Look at the birds of the air; they do not sow or reap or store away in barns, and yet your heavenly Father feeds them. Are you not much more valuable than they? Can any one of you by worrying add a single hour to your life?*
>
> *And why do you worry about clothes? See how the flowers of the field grow. They do not labor or spin. Yet I tell you that not even Solomon in all his splendor was dressed like one of these. If that is how God clothes the grass of the field, which is here today and tomorrow is thrown into the fire, will he not much more clothe you—you of little faith? So do not worry, saying, "What shall we eat?" or "What shall we drink?" or "What shall we wear?" For the pagans run after all these things, and your heavenly Father knows that you need them. But seek first his kingdom and his righteousness, and all these things will be given to you as well.*
>
> **—Matthew 6:25–33**

The key is to "seek first" the kingdom of God and let God handle the rest.

Jesus taught it, and Paul lived it. We often wonder if it's possible, but the Apostle Paul "learned the secret of being content" (Philippians 4:11–12).

Can you really be content regardless of the circumstances? Well, when Paul wrote about his contentment, he was writing from a prison cell. He was in a life-or-death situation, yet he had joy! Life wasn't working out as he had planned, but he shared Christ daily with the prison guards.

Paul wrote, "Rejoice in the Lord always. I will say it again: Rejoice!" (Philippians 4:4). Even in prison, Paul rejoiced! God wants us to have joy in our lives! Kids seem to laugh much more often than adults do. When did we lose our joy? This needs to change, and the change begins when we look to our sovereign, God, and realize that He is ultimately in control. We then choose to be people of joy. The Bible says, "A cheerful heart is good medicine" (Proverbs 17:22a). I like how the Westminster Shorter Catechism of 1647 sums it up: "Man's chief end is to glorify God, and to enjoy him forever."[20]

Keys to Contentment

We all want contentment. We want to live our lives without wrestling, striving, and struggling for more while never arriving. Paul said that he learned how to be content in every circumstance. How? "I can do all things through Christ who strengthens me" (Philippians 4:13 NKJV). This is the secret to contentment. Jesus is with you! But you must grow in your personal relationship with Jesus Christ. There's a difference between knowing about Jesus and knowing Jesus. There are a lot of people in the world who know about Jesus.

Bernhard Langer, World Golf Hall of Famer, had money, fame, cars—everything that would make a person successful in this world. However, in an interview, Langer said that even with all of these things, he felt emptiness inside. Then he attended his first Bible study, and it was the major turning point for him. It became clear that what was missing from his life was a personal relationship with

God and Jesus Christ. This new relationship fulfills him, and he has never felt the emptiness again, though over thirty years have gone by.[21] Nothing in this world can fill our hearts with the contentment we crave; only Jesus can do that. So, how do we access the strength to get through life that Jesus offers us?

Pray every day. I know that life is busy, but if you don't pray every day, you're missing out on power that is available to you. As we noted before, the Bible says, "Cast all your anxiety on him because he cares for you" (1 Peter 5:7). When anxiety, worry, or fear comes, pray immediately.

Many times when fear comes, our response is to wonder how we're going to fix it. What if our first response were to give it to God? Prayer will change your heart and mind. Prayer isn't just talking. It's also listening. It's a holy exchange. God is doing something bigger, and He wants you to see it.

Focus on what Jesus has provided. Just like Paul and Bernhard Langer, you can learn the secret of being content. Nothing outside of Jesus can solve your problems. He has already given you so much. Joy comes when you focus on what you do have and not on what you don't have. Allow God to be enough for you. You have the King of kings and the Lord of lords!

Remember that God is with you. You're not in this life alone! You lack nothing with God as your shepherd. Through Jesus, you are a child of God. You may go through ups and downs, but God is always with you, and your eternity is secure. You are forever His! We live in a broken world, but God is with you. He has also provided you with community to walk with you through the ups and downs of life.

Don't Do Life Alone

So many try to fight alone, but God has provided community for you. In fact, you were created for community. The Bible says, "As iron sharpens iron, so one person sharpens another" (Proverbs 27:17). We all need four to seven close people in our lives. Reach out to your local church and get involved. Surround yourself with godly people! Be honest with them and get help from pastors, counselors, and doctors when needed.

Not only that, but as you get involved in community, ask others, "How are you *really* doing?" *Really.* If you have kids, you know that they crave your attention and connection and are so effortlessly genuine. Like children, we all want to connect with someone. Connect with people in your community.

Too often we try to fight life on our own, but we weren't created to do that. Lock arms with people you can trust and who will hold you accountable, people who will get in the trenches with you and pray. You'll become like the people you hang out with. Their character is going to rub off on you. Get in a place where people will encourage you and point you to the Word.

There is no shame in getting help. Any shame is just a ploy of the enemy. Don't fight your battle alone. Fight it with your pastors, parents, counselors, and friends.

Is It Well with Your Soul?

One of my spiritual heroes is Horatio Spafford.[22] He grew up in Chicago and inherited a lot of money from his parents. He was also a lay leader in his church, always serving and helping out. People loved being around this man. Everything was going great in his life until 1871. His son died at the age of two. Then the Great Chicago Fire of 1871 ruined him financially.

His business interests were further hit by the economic downturn of 1873, at which time he had planned to travel to Europe with his family on the SS *Ville du Havre*. In a late change of plans, he sent his family ahead while he was delayed on business concerning zoning problems following the Great Chicago Fire. While crossing the Atlantic Ocean, the ship carrying his family sank rapidly after a collision with a sea vessel, the *Loch Earn*. All four of Spafford's daughters died. His wife, Anna, survived and sent him the now-famous telegram that read, "Saved alone."

Shortly afterward, as Spafford traveled to meet his grieving wife, he passed the place where the ship had sunk. He asked the captain to stop there, over the place where he had lost his four children. This is where he was inspired to write the words of this beloved hymn:[23]

When peace like a river attendeth my way,
When sorrows like sea billows roll;
Whatever my lot, Thou has taught me to say,
"It is well, it is well with my soul."

God is with you in whatever you may go through in life. God is with you in the darkest valley. He is the One who prepares a table for you on the other side. There are incredible blessings in life, and there are also challenges that we all face. But remember, your eternity is secure!

God encourages us to trust Him. Ultimately, God will fulfill His plan for your life. You just need to be faithful to what God has called you to do, and He will accomplish His will in and through you!

WORKBOOK

Chapter Six Questions

Question: When was one time you worried about something but saw things work out in the end?

_____

_____

_____

_____

_____

_____

_____

_____

_____

_____

_____

Question: How do you try to take control over things you can't control? How can you release that to Jesus?

_____

_____

_____

_____

_____

_____

_____

_____

_____

_____

Question: What do you believe about God? Do you believe that He is good and loving or that He is a condemning judge? How does this belief impact your life?

_____

_____

_____

_____

_____

_____

_____

_____

_____

_____

_____

Question: What is your first response when fear, anxiety, and worry arise? Do you pray about your anxieties or dwell on them?

_____

_____

_____

_____

_____

_____

_____

_____

_____

_____

_____

_____

Question: How can you begin to bring them to God? In what ways are you living in discontent? How can you turn that into contentment?

_____

_____

_____

_____

_____

_____

_____

_____

_____

_____

_____

Action: One day, God will make all things right. Read about that day in Revelation 21 and take time to worship God for being the One who will restore all things to His intended design in the end.

Chapter Six Notes

_____

_____

_____

_____

_____

_____

_____

_____

_____

_____

_____

_____

_____

_____

_____

_____

_____

_____

_____

_____

_____

_____

_____

_____

CONCLUSION

Are Your Eyes Fixed on Jesus?

Writing this in the midst of the COVID-19 pandemic makes the realities of the suffering world even more evident. Our need for the Lord is so abundantly clear during this time.

I'm an extrovert, and I love people and being with them! I miss being able to meet in person. But I'm also thankful for the technology that allows us to meet virtually, because we need the Lord. We need worship, and we need prayer. As individuals, as churches, and as nations, we need to focus on Jesus and set our eyes on Him.

God has been at work, even in the uncharted waters of the coronavirus pandemic. People have been watching sermons online from home and making commitments to Christ. Families have been studying God's Word together in their homes.

In unfamiliar or unprecedented times, you realize how much you are loved, cared for, and known by God. In difficult seasons, God has a purpose for you. A woman in my church who works as a nurse told me during the pandemic,

"The church has completely transformed my relationship with God, and I'm so thankful I have people walking along beside me.... The freedom I feel over anxiety and fear has helped me put on my 'scrubs' of armor and do what I know I'm called to do."

The CDC has sought the help of local churches in serving communities during the pandemic. We're praying for what God is doing in our communities, country, and world during this time. We pray for the people impacted directly and personally. We pray for the doctors, nurses, and others giving hope on the front lines. And we pray for teachers and parents trying to adapt the way they educate and raise their children. Churches continue to lock arms and be the hands and feet of Christ during challenging times. Even as we move past COVID-19, we will face other challenges in this life.

Meeting Jesus

When our eyes are on the problems we face—on job markets, stock markets, and spreading pandemics—the problems get bigger. When our eyes focus on Jesus instead, our faith grows stronger.

This was true for people in the Bible, too. Think of Mary, the mother of Jesus, who brought Him into the world and saw Him crucified. She persisted in faith and became part of the early church.

Then there was Thomas the Apostle, sometimes known as "Doubting Thomas." Many of us experiencing the coronavirus pandemic can probably relate to Doubting Thomas. People are asking themselves and God, "Why is this happening?" We all have experienced questions and doubts in this life.

The fact is that we live in a broken world. God created a perfect world back in the beginning, in the garden of Eden. Adam and Eve were in a right relationship with each other and with God. Everything was great—for the first two chapters of the book of Genesis!

Then Adam and Eve made it about them: "We don't want to do it Your way anymore." In other words, they sinned, and the perfection of God's creation gave way to a broken world of death and decay. But God didn't give up on them. Praise God that He doesn't give up on us, either!

He sent Jesus to meet us where we are, in our place of total depravity. In the early days of the pandemic, some people were ready to fight their neighbor for the last package of toilet paper! But Jesus looks past our weaknesses and still loves us.

When we meet Jesus, a miracle happens in our lives. The disciples met the resurrected Jesus, and their lives were never the same.

On the evening of that first day of the week, when the disciples were together, with the doors locked for fear of the Jewish leaders, Jesus came and stood among them and said, "Peace be with you!"
—John 20:19

After Jesus died on the cross, His disciples locked their doors out of fear of the Jewish leaders. Fear gripped them! As the coronavirus pandemic spread, that described many of us, too: gripped by fear and seeking safety behind locked doors.

Then Jesus came among the disciples and said, in effect, "I'm here! You can stop being afraid." They saw His resurrected body. He showed them His hands and His side. The disciples were filled with joy! He told them again, "Peace be with you!" and sent them out into the world equipped with the Holy Spirit (John 20:21–23).

But Thomas wasn't with the other disciples when Jesus first returned. Maybe he was off somewhere having a crisis of faith. Before Jesus' crucifixion, Thomas had been so committed that he was even prepared to die with Jesus (John 11:16). He also tended to ask questions that led to profound statements by Jesus (John 14:5–7).

Thomas was with them the next time Jesus came. Even though the doors were locked, Jesus appeared and said for the third time, "Peace be with you!" (John 20:26). Because Thomas had told the other disciples that he needed to touch, not just see, the physical proof of Jesus' return (John 20:25), Jesus specifically invited Thomas to touch His hands and side (John 20:27).

In other words, Jesus invited Thomas to stop doubting and to believe. He knew exactly where Thomas was struggling—in his doubts and fears. Jesus meets us where we are. Then Thomas believed, and he addressed Jesus, "My Lord and my God!" (John 20:28). He didn't merely call Jesus a teacher, as Judas Iscariot would have. Thomas realized that the One who had conquered death was God.

Jesus then spoke to us through the corridors of time and said that we are especially blessed to believe in Him without seeing Him the way Thomas did (John 20:29).

Afterward, Jesus continued to appear to His disciples, and some of these encounters were recorded as evidence for us that God wants us to have abundant life, both here and in the life to come. Thomas and the other disciples met the resurrected Jesus, and I pray that you will, too.

Doubt, the Doorway of Faith

Doubt is not a sin. God created us with the capacity for doubt. When we receive scam emails asking us for personal info or money, doubt is definitely a good thing! But doubt can go too far if it obstructs good things.

When my daughter asked me how I know that God is real, I was excited because I knew that God was working in her life. In answer to her question, I compared God to the wind: you don't see the wind itself, but you can see its effects and know that it's real. About one year later, I baptized my daughter when she gave her life to Christ.

God's ways are not our ways. He reveals Himself to us over time. But He can also handle our questions. Our doubt can lead us to truth.

Think about the crisis of faith experienced by Job, who lost his family, livestock, and livelihood. His wife suggested that he "curse God and die" (Job 2:9), but Job refused and did not sin. He trusted in God and praised Him, even though he didn't understand his suffering.

In Psalm 73, King David raised the question of why those who do wicked things prosper. When he went to God's temple, however, he perceived eternity and put his trust in God (Psalm 73:16–17).

Mother Teresa had doubts, but she ultimately trusted God and His purposes, including His purpose for her.[24] As Jesus told the father whose son was possessed by a spirit that was afflicting him, "Everything is possible for one who believes" (Mark 9:23). Doubt is meant to draw you closer to God.

Thomas showed up for church, so to speak, and that's where God met him. God can meet us in church, too. Sometimes people hear a sermon and say afterward, "It was like the preacher read my mind!" Sometimes when people say that to me, I didn't even say the things they thought I said! That was God speaking directly to them because they showed up. Put yourself in a position to hear from God by bringing your doubt to Jesus. Doubt is not the opposite of faith; the opposite of faith is unbelief.

Now Is the Time for Faith

During the challenges of life, many people have asked, "God, where are You?" The answer: He is here.

Given humankind's weakness and tendency toward sin, instead of asking why bad things happen, I think it's more appropriate to ask: why *good* things? Yet the Bible assures us that "in all things God works for the good of those who love him" (Romans 8:28). We can place our hope, faith, and life in Jesus.

Doubt leads us to a point of commitment. Jesus met Thomas in his doubt, but there came a point where He said to stop doubting and believe. Don't let your doubt become a dead end that makes you miserable and causes you to pull away. At some point, you must make a decision:

belief or unbelief. We all believe in something. The way I see it, it takes a bigger leap of faith to believe that God *doesn't* exist and *didn't* create the universe. It would be much harder to believe that it's all a result of coincidence.

During times of hardship, like a pandemic, things that are superficial are stripped away. The distractions, even the good ones, are taken from us, and we realize that only God remains.

What do you believe about Jesus? Do you love Him, or do you only love His blessings? Are you putting your faith in His hands and making Him your shepherd?

Placing your faith and trust in God doesn't have to be complicated. A single mother recently passed along this note from her young son, who was struggling emotionally in the wake of his parents' divorce:

> I was crying last night like usual, but then I prayed, and it helped. Thank you for telling me about God.

This same child had also experienced a period of anxiety about his schoolwork, but his mother showed him how to pray so he could turn his worries and fears over to God. When God took away his anxieties, the boy learned the power of faith. He knew that he could trust God in other difficult circumstances, too. That's how we fight the pandemic of anxiety in our lives.

Putting off a decision to surrender your anxiety to God and live by faith *is* a decision. Don't wait until things settle down in life to get serious about your faith. Don't procrastinate about what God wants you to do and how He wants you to live. Don't kick the can down the road.

We live in a culture of anxiety, worry, and fear, but God doesn't want that to define us. He wants us not to be anxious about anything. God is sovereign, which means that He is in control of everything. When we learn to fix our eyes on Jesus and trust Him fully, we can have peace. This doesn't mean that we won't go through challenging times in life, but it does mean that we will always know God is with us. Changing the music of your life to Psalm 23 will provide continual reassurance that the Lord is your shepherd and you lack nothing. God is with you, and He loves you forever!

REFERENCES

Notes

1. Quote Investigator. "I Am an Old Man and Have Known a Great Many Troubles, but Most of Them Never Happened." 2013. https://quoteinvestigator.com/2013/10/04/never-happened/.

2. Spurgeon, Charles Haddon. *Treasury of David*. 1869. CreateSpace Independent Publishing Platform, 2015.

3. Benner, Jeff A. "What Is the Difference Between lord, Lord, and LORD?" Ancient Hebrew Research Center. https://www.ancient-hebrew.org/god-yhwh/difference-between-lord-Lord-and-LORD.htm.

4. Benner, "What Is the Difference Between lord, Lord, and LORD?"

5. Hoomans, Joel. "35,000 Decisions: The Great Choices of Strategic Leaders." The Leading Edge. March 20, 2015. https://go.roberts.edu/leadingedge/the-great-choices-of-strategic-leaders.

6. Ruscio, A. M., L. S. Hallion, C. C. W. Lim, et al. "Cross-sectional Comparison of the Epidemiology of DSM-5 Generalized Anxiety

Disorder Across the Globe." *JAMA Psychiatry* 74, no. 5 (2017), p. 465–475. doi:10.1001/jamapsychiatry.2017.0056.

7. Petersen, Andrea. "Anxiety Looks Different in Men." The Wall Street Journal. July 30, 2019. https://www.wsj.com/articles/anxiety-looks-different-in-men-11564494352.

8. Swenson, Richard A. *Margin: Restoring Emotional, Physical, Financial, and Time Reserves to Overloaded Lives.* 1st edition. NavPress, 2004.

9. Lewis, C. S. *The Problem of Pain.* HarperOne, 2001, p. 33.

10. *Life Application Bible (New International Version),* Psalm 4:7 (footnote). Tyndale House Publishers and Zondervan Publishing House, 1991.

11. Bennett, Jessica. "It's a New Morning for Jennifer Aniston." The New York Times. October 31, 2019. https://www.nytimes.com/2019/09/10/arts/television/jennifer-aniston-apple-morning-show.html.

12. Yasharoff, Hannah. "Justin Bieber Gets Candid About Past Drug Addiction, Getting Sober: I 'Felt Like I Was Dying'." USA Today. February 4, 2020. usatoday.com/story/entertainment/celebrities/2020/02/04/justin-bieber-drug-addiction-detailed-waking-up-popping-pills-getting-sober/4653541002/.

13. Martin, Michel. "Can Mo' Money Really Mean Mo' Problems?" NPR. https://www.npr.org/2012/05/08/152258879/can-mo-money-really-mean-mo-problems.

14. McManus, Harold. "Shepherding Practices of the First Century AD." *Biblical Illustrator* (Fall 1986): p. 79–81. https://margaretfeinberg.com/wp-content/uploads/2018/08/Scouting-Leader-Article_Shepherding-practices.pdf.

15. Tripp, Paul David. "February 26." In *New Morning Mercies: A Daily Gospel Devotional*. Crossway, 2014.

16. Morgan, Robert J. "What You Have When You Have Christ." March 19, 2017. Robert J. Morgan (blog). https://www.robertjmorgan.com/devotional/what-you-have-when-you-have-christ/.

17. American Psychiatric Association. "Americans Say They Are More Anxious Than a Year Ago; Baby Boomers Report Greatest Increase in Anxiety." May 7, 2018. https://www.psychiatry.org /newsroom/news-releases/americans-say-they-are-more-anxious-than-a-year-ago-baby-boomers-report-greatest-increase-in-anxiety.

18. McManus, "Shepherding Practices of the First Century AD."

19. A. W. Tozer. *The Knowledge of the Holy: The Attributes of God, Their Meaning in the Christian Life*. 1961. Clarke, 1965, p. 4.

20. "Shorter Catechism of the Assembly of Divines." 1648. A Puritan's Mind. Puritan Publications. https://www.apuritansmind.com/westminster-standards/shorter-catechism/.

21. Kingdom. "Bernhard Langer: Playing the Waiting Game." http://kingdom.golf/uncategorized/bernhard-langer-playing-the-waiting-game/.

22. "The American Colony in Jerusalem: Family Tragedy." Library of Congress. https://www.loc.gov/exhibits/americancolony/amcolony-family.html.

23. Spafford, Horatio Gates. "When Peace, Like a River." 1873. https://hymnary.org/text/when_peace_like_a_river_attendeth_my_w ay.

24. Mother Teresa. *Mother Teresa: Come Be My Light*. Edited by Brian Kolodiejchuk. Crown Publishing Group, 2007.

About the Author

Jeff Simmons is the founder and senior pastor of Rolling Hills Community Church in Franklin, Tennessee. He also serves as the president of Justice & Mercy International, a nonprofit that exists to make justice personal for the poor, the orphaned, and the forgotten of the world. He received his bachelor's from Baylor University and his master's from Southwestern Theological Seminary. Jeff's faith in God, and his roles as a husband and as a father to three daughters, motivate him to be the leader he is and to do the work to which he has been called.

Website: www.jeffsimmons.org
Instagram: @_jeffsimmons
Twitter: @_jeffsimmons
Facebook: @RHCCJeffSimmons

About Sermon To Book

SermonToBook.com began with a simple belief: that sermons should be touching lives, *not* collecting dust. That's why we turn sermons into high-quality books that are accessible to people all over the globe.

Turning your sermon series into a book exposes more people to God's Word, better equips you for counseling, accelerates future sermon prep, adds credibility to your ministry, and even helps make ends meet during tight times.

John 21:25 tells us that the world itself couldn't contain the books that would be written about the work of Jesus Christ. Our mission is to try anyway. Because in heaven, there will no longer be a need for sermons or books. Our time is now.